THE SPICE OF AMERICA

THE
GOOD
TIME
LIBRARY

THE SPICE OF AMERICA

by JUNE SWANSON

illustrated by

PRISCILLA KIEDROWSKI

Carolrhoda Books, Inc. · Minneapolis

LIBRARY OF CONGRESS CATALOGING IN PUBLICATION DATA

Swanson, June.
  The spice of America.

  (The Good time library)
  Summary: Traces the little-known origins of such
American phenomena as the doughnut, Mary's little lamb,
the beaver hat, the Ferris wheel, the Raggedy Ann doll,
and denim jeans.
  1. United States—History—Anecdotes, facetiae,
satire, etc.—Juvenile literature. [1. United States—
History—Miscellanea. 2. United States—Civilization—
Miscellanea] I. Kiedrowski, Priscilla, ill. II. Title.
E178.4.S9 1983   973   83-5298
ISBN 0-87614-252-8 (lib . bdg.)

1 2 3 4 5 6 7 8 9 10 91 90 89 88 87 86 85 84 83

To all those people
who have added the spice

A history book is like a meal. It's the meat and potatoes of a country's story. But to keep any meal interesting, spices must be added. The fifteen stories in this book are just that—the spices that bring out the flavor of America's past.

Contents

>·<

I

The State that Isn't

If someone asked you how many states are in the United States, of course you would answer 50, and of course you'd be right. With a little change in the events of history, though, you might have had to say 51 to be correct.

At one time there almost *was* another state. It was named Franklin in honor of Benjamin Franklin. Franklin existed for four years, from 1784 until 1788. During those four years it had its own governor and its own constitution.

Franklin's story began in June of 1784. The state of North Carolina felt it had too much territory to take care of, so it gave some of its western land back to the federal government. But Congress was slow in voting to accept the return of this land. When November came and Congress still had not acted on the offer, North Carolina changed its mind. It decided it wanted to keep the land after all.

From June to November the land did not legally belong to North Carolina, nor did it belong to the federal government. This meant that the people who lived there were left without protection from either government. Unfortunately, relations between white people and Indians were not good in that area, and the whites needed help from their government. They decided they had to do something.

Some of the leading citizens of the region met in Jonesboro (now in the state of Tennessee) in August and again in December of 1784. They wanted a government, and they wanted protection from the Indians. They decided in those meetings to make their orphan territory into a new state which would be called Franklin.

In order to become a state, a territory must be recognized as such by the U.S. Congress. This hadn't happened yet, but the people of Franklin didn't care. They immediately began to act as if Franklin really were a state. They elected John Sevier as its governor. Sevier was a North Carolina pioneer who had fought the British in the American Revolution and had led campaigns against the Cherokee Indians. Other state officials were also appointed. Because Franklin had little money, these officials were usually paid in furs, whiskey, or tobacco.

The next year, 1785, Franklin purchased additional land from the Cherokee Indians in the Treaty of Dumplin Creek and created four new counties. More than ever the people of Franklin wanted their territory to become a state, so they sent a representative to Congress to ask for this recognition. But by then, of course, North

Carolina had changed its mind. Its governor, Josiah Martin, called the new state unlawful, and Congress turned down Franklin's request.

The area was caught in a tug-of-war between the Franklin supporters and the government of North Carolina. Both sides

tried to rule the land. Taxes were charged by both governments. Each government tried to enforce its own laws and operated its own set of courts. As if this weren't enough trouble, Franklin's citizens were fighting among themselves over land ownership, and the government of Franklin

was becoming weaker and weaker.

Then North Carolina elected a new governor, Richard Caswell, who was determined to solve Franklin's problems with North Carolina. Apparently he was successful, because when Sevier's term as governor ended in 1788, the people of Franklin did not hold an election to replace him. North Carolina regained control of the area, and Franklin's four-year struggle to become a state ended.

Two years later, in 1790, North Carolina gave the same land to the federal government again! This time it became a part of the new "Territory of the United States South of the River Ohio," and in 1796 it was admitted to the Union as a part of the state of Tennessee. The people elected John Sevier, the old governor of Franklin, as the first governor of Tennessee. He served six terms as governor and was then elected to the state senate for one term. He later served in Congress until his death.

If things had been just a little different

—if North Carolina had not wanted the land back, if Franklin's government had been a little stronger, if Congress had acted sooner to accept the land from North Carolina, or if Congress had later decided to recognize the new state in spite of North Carolina's objections—there might be 51 states today.

II

How Did the Hole Get There?

When early settlers from Holland came to the New World, they brought along a love for deep fried foods. Dutch housewives were famous for their fried cakes, called *olykoecks*, and it was from this *olykoeck* that a new food developed—the all-American doughnut!

The doughnut is very much like the old fried cake except for the hole in its center. How did the hole get there, and how did the "nut" get in the name? There are about as many answers to these questions as there are doughnuts in a bakery. Some of them make good stories, but only one is true.

Would you believe this one? One day a Dutch housewife was making fried cakes in the kitchen of her frontier home. An Indian crept up and shot an arrow through the kitchen window. As fate would have it, the arrow sailed right through the center of a cake she was about to drop into the frying pan, and there was the first doughnut!

How about this one? The word doughnut came into being during the First World War. The Red Cross served so many to our "doughboys" (as American soldiers were called) that the cakes were named "doughnuts" after the soldiers.

Or this one: New England sailors used to enjoy fried cakes while they were standing watch at the wheel. When they got busy and needed both hands, they would spear the cakes on the spokes of the wheel. One clever captain, wanting to help his crew, had the cook make fried cakes with the holes already in them, and the first doughnut was invented.

There's just one more story. It goes like this. From the earliest days of the United States, the men of Maine were sailors and fishermen. Maine's long coastline and its thick inland forests produced a booming shipbuilding industry. Soon many towns along the coast of the state became shipping centers.

From this Maine background came a

sea captain named Hanson Gregory. Now Captain Gregory's mother was an excellent cook. She was always trying new recipes for him to use aboard his ship. One of her specialties was a fried cake. Because the dough in the middle of these cakes didn't always cook all the way through, their centers were often doughy, so Mrs. Gregory started putting a walnut or a hazelnut in each center. It was because of this nut center that she called her cakes "dough*nuts.*"

Her doughnuts were a favorite of Captain Gregory and his crew. However, nuts were expensive and often hard to get. One day in 1847, when the good captain was in port, he asked a tinsmith to make a circular cutter with a small hole in the center. His mother tried the new cutter and found that with it her doughnuts fried perfectly —no soggy centers and no more expensive nuts. Ever after that, Mrs. Gregory made her famous doughnuts with a hole in the middle.

Which is the true story? The last one.

III

The White House

On June 18, 1812, President James Madison approved an act of Congress declaring war on Great Britain. The British had been stopping American ships on the high seas and illegally searching them. They often carried off American sailors who they claimed were deserters from the British navy. The United States felt it had to put a stop to this, so Congress declared war.

In the summer of 1814, a British fleet sailed into the Chesapeake Bay. A large party of soldiers went ashore. The American forces were not strong enough to hold them back, and the British were soon marching on Washington, D.C. They burned much of the city, including the Capitol building, the Library of Congress, and the president's house.

President Madison was away at the time on an inspection tour of American troops, but through the bravery and quick thinking of his wife, Dolley, many of America's historical documents and other items were saved. Into an old wagon she loaded her husband's official papers, the original Declaration of Independence (which had been framed and placed under glass), silver from the dining room, and a famous portrait of George Washington painted by Gilbert Stuart.

Dolley Madison then dressed herself and her maid in clothes that a farmer's wife and her servant might have worn. She took along a friend and a soldier who also dressed as farmers. In this way they were able to leave the burning city in safety.

After the burning of Washington, D.C.,

the British moved on to Baltimore, but that city was defended by Fort McHenry. Both the British army and the British naval fleet were driven back, and Baltimore was saved.

As soon as it was safe, members of the U.S. government returned to Washington, and President Madison ordered the rebuilding of the city. The president's house had been badly burned. Only the blackened shell of its walls remained standing. The house probably would have been completely destroyed if the fire hadn't been put out by a summer thunderstorm during the night of the burning.

As it was, the president's house had to be rebuilt practically from the bottom up. The inside had been totally destroyed, and all of the furnishings were gone. The rebuilding took almost four years.

For a few months the Madisons lived in a private house just west of the old president's house. Then in 1815 they moved to a house on the corner of Pennsylvania

Avenue and 19th Street, where they lived until the end of Madison's term of office.

When James Monroe became president in 1817, the house still was not ready. The Monroes lived in their own house in Washington for nine months. Finally the president's house was finished, and on New Year's Day in 1818, President and Mrs. Monroe held a reception to reopen it. At that time its name was officially declared to be the Executive Mansion.

Because workmen had applied numerous coats of white paint to hide the smoke-blackened walls, the outside of the Executive Mansion was now a dazzling white. For this reason, in spite of its new official name, it was often called simply the white house.

Its official name changed several times throughout the next 80 years, to the President's Mansion, the President's Home, and even the President's Palace. To most people, though, it was still the white house.

Then in 1902 President Theodore Roosevelt authorized this popular name as the official title of the president's home, and it has been the White House ever since.

IV

An Official Thanksgiving

The first national Thanksgiving Day in the United States was proclaimed by George Washington for November 26, 1789. He called it a day of general thanksgiving for the adoption of the new Constitution. But it wasn't until 1863, 74 years later, that the second national Thanksgiving Day was proclaimed by Abraham Lincoln.

During the time in between, many states began to celebrate their own Thanksgiving Days, but the dates differed from state to state. What happened to the *national* holiday during those 74 years? The answer to that can be found in the story of one woman—Sarah Buell Hale. Born in 1788, Sarah was one year old when George Washington set that first Thanksgiving Day. She was 75 before the next national Thanksgiving was celebrated, and to a great extent Sarah Hale was the reason it *was* celebrated again nationally.

Sarah Hale's life was not an easy one. When her husband died, she was left with five small children to support. To make money Sarah turned to writing poems, essays, and finally a novel. Because of her writing, she was asked to edit the first magazine published just for women, *The Ladies' Magazine*. Later she became the editor of *Godey's Lady's Book*, a position she held for 40 years.

During this time, tension was building between the northern states and the southern states. Sarah Hale was upset by the feeling of unrest throughout the country. She felt that what was needed was a national day of thanksgiving—a day that would unite the entire country, north and

south, in prayer and praise of God.

In her magazine, Sarah wrote:

> The unifying effect of such a festival can hardly be overrated. The pulpits, during the day, one in every year, will be occupied with the stirring incidents of national history.... The people of our country will learn to value the bond of national union when they know with what mighty labors and sacrifices it was wrought.

It was this love of country that Sarah wanted the people to celebrate. At another time she wrote that the holiday would be "a pledge of love and loyalty to the Constitution of the United States, which guarantees peace, prosperity and perpetuity to our great Republic."

For years Sarah wrote letters to congressmen, governors, and even presidents, asking them to support such a day. She gave countless speeches to any group who would listen to her. She used her magazine to persuade women of the need for such a holiday. She even printed recipes to use in preparing meals for a Thanksgiving Day dinner.

By the beginning of the Civil War in 1861, 29 states and territories were celebrating a common Thanksgiving Day, but it still was not a national holiday. Seeing the suffering caused by the bitter war made Sarah fight even harder for her holiday. She wrote letter after letter to President Lincoln until he finally proclaimed a second national Thanksgiving Day for November 26, 1863.

Still Sarah was not completely satisfied. She wanted to make sure there would be a national Thanksgiving Day every year, so she wrote even more letters. Some reports say that she even visited President Lincoln.

Finally President Lincoln set the last Thursday in November as an annual national Thanksgiving Day, but he didn't make it a *legal* holiday, a day on which no government business is conducted. In 1941 Congress changed the date to the fourth Thursday in November and declared Thanksgiving a legal holiday.

Today, thanks to Sarah Buell Hale and her one-woman campaign, the United States has an official Thanksgiving Day every November.

V

Mary Had a Little Lamb

The same Sarah Hale who fought for Thanksgiving Day is also said to have written the poem, "Mary Had a Little Lamb." In 1830 the verse was printed in a small collection of poems edited by Mrs. Hale. According to the *real* Mary, though, the first 12 lines were written by John Roulstone. It is thought that Sarah Hale may have added the additional verses.

Yes, there really was a Mary—Mary Elizabeth Sawyer—and she really did have a lamb. Mary Sawyer was born in Sterling, Massachusetts, on March 22, 1806.

One cold spring day, when she was about

nine years old, Mary found a new-born lamb that had been abandoned by its mother. The lamb was very weak. Mary asked her father if she might take it into the house to try to save it. Her father told her not to bother; the lamb would probably die anyway. But Mary insisted and finally was allowed to keep the lamb.

She held it in her arms all that first night, keeping it warm and feeding it. Day after day she cared for it. Soon the lamb was strong enough to stand and then to walk. It became Mary's pet and followed her everywhere. That's how it happened to follow Mary and her brother to school one day. Fortunately they arrived before the teacher did, so Mary covered the lamb with a blanket and tucked it under her seat. There it slept quietly until Mary walked to the front of the room to recite. Then the lamb jumped out of its hiding place and followed her down the aisle. Of course everyone laughed, and the teacher asked Mary to put her lamb outside. It

waited by the door until Mary could take it home.

There was a visitor at school that day, a young man named John Roulstone. The next day he rode up to the school and handed Mary a piece of paper on which he had written:

> Mary had a little lamb,
> Its fleece was white as snow,
> And every-where that Mary went,
> The lamb was sure to go.
> It followed her to school one day,
> That was against the rule;
> It made the children laugh and play
> To see a lamb at school.
> And so the teacher turned it out;
> But still it lingered near,
> And waited patiently about,
> Till Mary did appear.

Mary loved the poem. She often gave copies of it to her friends. No one knows for certain if it was because of these copies or because of its publication in Sarah Hale's book that the poem became so well known.

From the lamb's first wool Mary's mother made her two pairs of stockings. Mary kept these stockings to remind her of her beloved pet. Many years later she gave the stockings to a group that was raising money to save the Old South Meeting House in Boston. The stockings were unraveled, and pieces of yarn were attached to cards that Mary signed. Everyone wanted a piece of wool from Mary's lamb, and the cards sold well.

Even Thomas Edison remembered the poem when he was inventing the phonograph. The very first words ever heard on a phonograph were, "Mary had a little lamb."

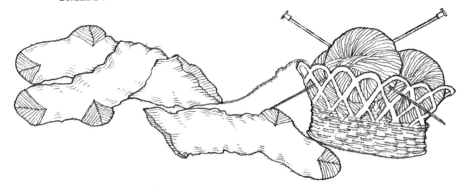

VI

Leave It to Beavers

Today we seldom see a beaver running across our lawns or even swimming in a nearby lake, but hundreds of years ago there were countless wild beavers all over North America. These small animals played an important part in the building of the United States.

Their importance began because of the fashions of Europe. The wide-brimmed, plumed hats that were once so popular in the courts of Europe were made of a soft material known as felt, and in those days felt was made from beaver fur. If you were to look at a piece of beaver hair under a microscope, you would see tiny, over-lapping scales on it. When these hairs are pressed together with steam or hot water, the scales blend together and form felt.

By the sixteenth century, beavers in Europe had been so hunted for their fur that there were very few of them left. So when European explorers came to the New World, they were excited by the large number of beavers they saw. Soon the French, English, and Dutch were all com-peting for this fur trade.

In 1608 a French explorer, Samuel de Champlain, started a fur-trading post in Canada on the St. Lawrence River. He called the post Quebec. Indians came to the trading post in canoes loaded with beaver furs which they traded for beads, metal goods, and weapons.

When the beaver began to disappear from this region, Champlain built another post farther west near the Huron Indian village of Hochelaga. A few years later a fort was built there by Catholic missionaries from France. It was called Montreal Fort, and it soon became a prosperous fur-trading center. From this fur-trading fort grew the present city of Montreal. The lowly beaver had been responsible for starting two of Canada's largest cities.

The English were also pushing west from the Atlantic coast, looking for ways to increase their beaver trade. In the spring of 1610 the British sent Henry Hudson to explore the land west of Fort Montreal. He discovered a large bay, which was promptly named Hudson Bay.

There the English started the powerful Hudson's Bay Company to trade with the Indians for furs. The company built forts and trading posts around the shore of the bay and sent agents far into the wilderness to trade with the Indians. It was not long before they were trading with Indians all the way from Hudson Bay to the Pacific Ocean. Now the beaver had not only helped to found two great Canadian cities, it had also helped to open up the country from coast to coast.

Fur traders were also pushing across the land south of the Canadian border—land that would someday be called the United States. They built forts and trading posts along the upper Mississippi and upper Missouri rivers.

Two French fur traders, Pierre LacLede Liguest and Rene Auguste Chouteau, began a fur-trading post on the Mississippi River in 1764. They named it St. Louis after a French king, Louis IX, who had been made a saint. The trading post of St. Louis soon became the fur center for the newly developing region. Thus the little beaver was responsible for starting yet another great city—St. Louis, Missouri.

From St. Louis, trappers and fur traders fanned out into the Rocky Mountains and the southwestern deserts, opening up lands that had never before been seen by white people. They pushed across the Sierra mountains to reach the settlements of California. All the while they were searching for more beavers.

The beaver trade prospered until about
1835. By then much of the beaver population in America had disappeared, just as
it had years before in Europe. Fortunately,
about that same time, silk hats were
coming into fashion in Paris, and their
popularity soon reached London, Montreal,
and New York. People no longer wanted
beaver hats, so the demand for beaver fell,
and the beaver had a much better chance
of survival. Today we hardly remember
that this little animal helped to open up
a whole continent.

VII

The Ferris Wheel

Can you imagine a fair or a carnival without a Ferris wheel standing out over everything else? No fair would be complete without one.

Today's Ferris wheels are normally 40 to 60 feet tall, which may seem high when you're on the top looking down, but the very first Ferris wheel was 250 feet high. That's taller than a 20-story building! This huge Ferris wheel was built for the 1893 World's Fair, the Columbian Exposition, in Chicago. The backers of the fair were looking for a special attraction— something that would be sure to draw

people to the fair. The Eiffel Tower had been a great success for the Paris fair of 1889, and Chicagoans wanted something to equal that tower for their fair. They challenged American civil engineers to come up with something.

George Washington Gale Ferris submitted an idea to the fair backers for a giant wheel on which people could ride. Everyone laughed at his idea at first. They thought it was impossible. But Ferris managed to raise enough money to start the Ferris Wheel Company, and he began to make plans and gather material for his wheel. Finally he was able to convince the people who ran the fair that his idea would work and that he would be able to construct the giant wheel in time for the fair.

No mill or machine shop in the country was large enough to make the entire wheel, so Ferris had to have it built in pieces by small shops. The pieces were to be assembled right at the fairground. Each

piece had to fit exactly; there could be
no mistakes. It took ironworkers all spring
to put together the first Ferris wheel.

A Ferris wheel today usually has 12 to
16 seats that hold 2 or 3 people each,
but that first one had 36 enclosed cars that
each carried 60 passengers. When filled,
it carried 2,160 people at one time!

Six platforms were used to load and unload passengers. Each ride was two full turns of the wheel. On the first turn, the wheel made six stops to load passengers. The second turn was a non-stop, nine-minute ride. Each car had five large, glass windows giving everyone a spectacular view of Chicago and Lake Michigan.

The first Ferris wheel finally opened in June of 1893 and proved to be one of the most popular attractions at the fair. During that summer in Chicago, 1,500,000 people rode the Ferris wheel.

After the fair the ride was moved to a nearby amusement park. In 1904 it was moved again, this time to St. Louis for the Louisiana Purchase Exposition. After the St. Louis fair closed, the wheel stood unused for two years. Then in 1906 it was sold to a wrecking company for scrap metal. It took 200 pounds of dynamite to dismantle it.

Fortunately for Ferris wheel fans, a Chicago bridge builder, W. E. Sullivan, figured out how to make a smaller wheel that could be taken apart and put together easily. In 1906 he started the Big Eli Bridge Company, and this company still makes most of the Ferris wheels used today.

VIII

A Jinx?

At breakfast on the morning of April 15, 1865, Abraham Lincoln mentioned that he and Mrs. Lincoln were going to the theater that evening. He asked his son Robert to join them. They would be attending a performance of *Our American Cousins* at the Ford Theater.

Robert had to turn down the invitation; he had already made other plans for the evening. It was a decision he regretted for the rest of his life, for that night at the theater President Lincoln was shot by John Wilkes Booth. Robert felt that if only he had been there, he might have been able to do something that would have prevented his father's assassination.

After the activities surrounding his father's death had quieted down, Robert returned to Harvard Law School and later became a successful lawyer. When James Garfield was elected president, he asked Robert to be his secretary of war, so Lincoln became a member of Garfield's cabinet.

On the Fourth of July weekend in 1881, Garfield invited Robert Lincoln to join him for a trip to his twenty-fifth college reunion. Lincoln arrived at the railroad station just in time to see Garfield shot. The president died several weeks later. Once again a presidential assassination had closely touched the life of Robert Lincoln.

When his duties as secretary of war were finished, Lincoln returned to his law practice in Chicago. He became a legal counselor for the Pullman Railroad Company and in time became its president and chairman of the board. An important

ABRAHAM
LINCOLN

JAMES
GARFIELD

WILLIAM
McKINLEY

citizen of the country, Lincoln was invited to be one of the officials to open the Pan American Exposition in Buffalo, New York. The year was 1901. President William McKinley was also in Buffalo to open the fair and to give a speech.

Everyone was in a happy mood on the opening day of the exposition. As Lincoln joined the other officials in the presidential party, they were surrounded by a group of people who wanted to shake the president's hand. No one noticed that a man with a bandaged hand had joined the line of hand-shakers. The bandage was actually a handkerchief concealing a gun. As President McKinley reached out to shake the man's hand, two shots were heard. Eight days later, McKinley died— the third U.S. president to be assassinated by a gunman.

From that day on, Lincoln refused to attend any public gathering with a president of the United States. "And they had better not invite me," he said, "because there is a certain fatality about presidential functions when I am present."

Robert Lincoln felt he was a jinx.

IX

The Making of a President

In 1826 Eliza McCardle was a 16-year-old schoolteacher in the small town of Greenville, Tennessee. In September of that year a young man came to town. He set up business and hung out a sign announcing, "A. Johnson, tailor."

Eliza set out at once to learn more about this handsome newcomer. Soon the two had met and become good friends. The young tailor was 18, and his name was Andrew. He and his mother lived in the small room behind his shop. His father had died when he was three, leaving his mother to support the family. The young mother had taken in washing and sewing to make ends meet. As soon as Andrew had been old enough, his mother had apprenticed him to a tailor. To Eliza McCardle's dismay, she learned that Andrew had never been to school and was struggling to teach himself to read.

To Eliza this was unthinkable. No man could possibly make anything of his life if he couldn't read or write. Whenever possible, she tried to help the young tailor. Besides reading and writing, she taught him arithmetic, history, government, and geography. Andrew had a special interest in politics, and Eliza began to read newspapers to him. He enjoyed hearing the latest news from Washington and from the state capital, Nashville.

As Andrew's education progressed, so did his and Eliza's romance. On May 17, 1827, Eliza and Andrew were married. She was 17, and he had not yet turned 19.

Andrew had saved enough money to buy a small farm for his mother, and

he and Eliza moved into the room behind the tailor shop. Now Eliza spent every free minute teaching her husband. In the evenings she read to him as he stitched. Andrew's ambitions grew as he learned more of the world. He realized that he did not want to be a tailor for the rest of his life.

Andrew was a good speaker. He had a powerful voice and a quick mind. The young men of the village often came to the shop to talk with him and hear his views on the news of the day. He became much admired by the working people of Greenville. When a debating society was started at a nearby college, he became one of its most active members. Several times a week he walked four miles to take part in the debates.

Andrew and Eliza were thrifty and hard-working. Soon they were able to buy a house of their own, and little by little they bought other property. At the age of 20 Andrew was elected alderman. At 22 he became mayor of Greenville. Both times he was elected as a representative of the Workingman's Party.

This was only the beginning. With Eliza's help and encouragement he went to Nashville as a representative to the state legislature. Next he was elected to Congress, and in 1853 he became governor of Tennessee. By then he was 45 years old.

Finally, in 1864, Andrew Johnson was elected as Abraham Lincoln's vice president. When President Lincoln was killed, Johnson, a man who had never been to school, became the president of the United States.

Andrew Johnson probably would never have made that long journey from tailor to president without Eliza McCardle, his teacher, his wife, and his loyal supporter.

X

Marcella's Old Rag Doll

One day in the early 1900s a little girl named Marcella Gruelle was playing in the attic of her grandmother's house in Indiana. There she found a rag doll that her grandmother had made many years earlier for Marcella's Aunt Prudence.

Marcella brought the old doll downstairs. Her grandmother repaired it and washed its clothes. Marcella's father, Johnny, was an artist. He painted a new face on the doll. It looked as good as new.

Johnny Gruelle had begun his art career at the age of 19 doing political cartoons for the *Indianapolis Sun*. From there he went to work for the *Cleveland Press*. In 1910 he moved his family to New York, where he drew illustrations for a number of magazines. In 1914 he illustrated his first book, *Grimm's Complete Fairy Tales*.

In the meantime, the old rag doll became one of Marcella's favorite toys. It moved with the family to Cleveland and then to New York. But Marcella was to live in New York only a short time. She died in 1916 at the age of 14.

To help ease his grief Johnny kept Marcella's old rag doll on his desk where he could see it every day. He thought about his daughter often. Finally he decided to write and illustrate a book about Marcella and her rag doll. He named the doll after two of his favorite poems by James Whitcomb Riley, "The Raggedy Man" and "Little Orphan Annie." Right there in Johnny's office the old rag doll became Raggedy Ann.

When the book *Raggedy Ann Stories* was published in 1918, the old rag doll was put on display to promote book sales. She was such a hit that Marcella's grandmother and her Aunt Prudence were asked to make more dolls to sell. The two women made and stuffed by hand hundreds of Raggedy Anns. The dolls sold faster than the two women could make them, and when the demand became too great, it was decided to have the dolls made commercially.

In 1920 Johnny created a brother doll named Raggedy Andy. The two dolls became the subjects of many more of his books.

Since that time, countless Raggedy Anns have been made. They remain popular today, and they have changed very little from that original old rag doll. They still have the same loops of red yarn for hair, the same shoe-button eyes, and the same contagious smile. They still wear a calico dress, a white pinafore, pantaloons, and red-and-white striped stockings. And because of the candy heart that was sewn

inside the Raggedy Ann in the original *Raggedy Ann Stories*, all Raggedy Anns still wear a painted heart that says, "I LOVE YOU."

Not only are Raggedy Ann *dolls* popular, today Raggedy's smiling face can be seen on jewelry, bedspreads, games, calendars, dishes, lamps, watches, stationery, radios, sleeping bags, and more. The list is endless. At Expo '67 in Canada, Raggedy Ann had the honor of being named the classic American folk doll.

XI

The Fisk Jubilee Singers

At the end of the Civil War, the American Missionary Association helped found Fisk University near Nashville, Tennessee. It was started as a school for ex-slaves. The old Union army barracks outside of Nashville were made into classrooms and dormitories for the students.

From the beginning the new university was short of money. In order to buy books, rusty handcuffs and fetters from the old slave pens were sold for scrap metal.

Hoping to raise money for the school, the music teacher, George L. White, organized a small group of singers to put on concerts. The group was called the Fisk Jubilee Singers after the Old Testament's "Year of the Jubilee," which marked the end of the Jews' bondage in Egypt. Only a short time before, these singers had been in bondage too.

Ella Sheppard, the group's pianist, wrote, "Taking every cent he had, all the school treasury could spare, and all he could borrow, Mr. White started in God's strength, October 6, 1871, to sing the money out of the hearts and pockets of the people."

At first the group had very small audiences. They sang popular "white man's music" like "Home, Sweet Home." But their performance at a religious conference in Oberlin, Ohio, changed all that. That evening they sang only one song—one of the old slave songs—called "Steal Away to Jesus." The audience was deeply touched by the beauty of the song.

From then on the Fisk chorus sang little besides these old slave songs, or, as they are known today, spirituals. These songs made a deep impression on white audiences, but still the concerts brought in little money.

When they got to New York City, though, ministers helped to arrange large audiences for them, and they received many gifts for the new school as well as money. Next they went to New England. There the singers were even more successful. One week in Connecticut brought in $3,900 for Fisk University.

As their tour progressed, the singers became more and more famous. They even sang "Go Down, Moses" at the White House for President Grant.

After their appearance at the White House, the Fisk Jubilee Singers began the first of two tours of Europe, where they immediately won the hearts of the people. They sang in hospitals, in prisons, and in the streets. They sang for Queen Victoria, the queen of England at that time.

One night they were invited to dinner at the home of the prime minister of England.

All the servants were dismissed. The prime minister and his wife wanted the honor of serving the ex-slaves themselves.

The crown princess of Germany was said to have cried when she heard them sing "Nobody Knows the Trouble I See." In Holland they could barely walk down the streets for the children pressing close to them.

When they came home from Europe, Fisk University was $150,000 richer, but the music of the world was the real winner. It, too, was made richer by these spirituals. Without the Fisk Jubilee Singers, the old slave songs might have been lost forever.

XII

Bank by Mail

When someone says, "bank by mail," we think of putting checks into envelopes and mailing them to the bank, but to the people of Vernal, Utah, in 1918, the words had a different meaning. The Bank of Vernal was *built* by mail. Each of its 80,000 bricks came from Salt Lake City by mail!

In the early 1900s more and more farmers, ranchers, and miners were moving into the area around Vernal. The town soon became a trading center and a larger bank was needed. An architect was hired to design the new building. He felt that the outside of the bank should be built with special bricks made by the Pressed Brick Company in Salt Lake City.

Vernal is only 125 miles from Salt Lake City, but there was no railroad between the two cities, and the road was little more than a path over the mountains. The cost of bringing the bricks by wagon over the mountain trail would have been several times the cost of the bricks themselves. If the bank was to be built, a cheaper way had to be found to deliver the bricks.

Then someone discovered that mail rates in the area were figured by drawing circles on a map using Salt Lake City as the center. Areas within the inner circles, close to Salt Lake City, paid lower postal rates than areas farther out. Vernal fell within one of the inner circles and was therefore entitled to cheaper mail rates— no matter how roundabout the way might be to get there.

So the bricks were ordered. The Pressed

Brick Company in Salt Lake City was told to pack the bricks in 50-pound packages and mail them to the bank in Vernal.

The packages had to go almost 400 miles to reach Vernal. First they traveled by train 265 miles to Mack, Colorado. There they were put on a smaller train that took them another 60 miles back to Watson, Utah. At Watson they were loaded onto freight wagons for the last 65 miles. The wagon trip took four days and included crossing the Green River by ferry.

For a while this brick mailing worked just fine. Then the postmaster in Salt Lake City began to worry about the large shipments to Vernal. He sent a telegram to the postmaster general in Washington, D.C., asking what he should do. The postmaster general immediately made a new regulation that forbade any individual or company from mailing more than 200 pounds to one person in one day.

By then tons and tons of bricks were already on the way to Vernal. They were

exempt from the new regulation since they had already been mailed, but there were still tons more to be shipped that would not be exempt. Again someone had an idea. The brick company began addressing the 50-pound packages to different people in Vernal. Townspeople and ranchers alike picked up their shipments of bricks from the post office and carried them to the site of the new bank.

Everyone in Vernal was glad to help because everyone wanted the bank. The ranchers in particular thought this parcel post delivery was a great idea. It was inexpensive, fast, and reliable. Soon they were ordering all sorts of things by mail. They even began to mail their crops to market. One shipment of corn was said to have needed ten four-ton mail trucks to carry it. Needless to say, parcel post regulations were changed soon after this!

In short order the Bank of Vernal was completed. The original building is still being used today, although it has been expanded and is now called Zion's First National Bank.

XIII

Mountain Men

Just as beavers were partly responsible for opening up the American continent, "mountain men" trappers were partly responsible for opening up the western mountains. In their footsteps followed miners, cowboys, and settlers.

It was easy to spot a mountain man. His clothes were made of buckskin, fringed at the seams. He wore a low-crowned, wool hat or one he had made from fur. His boots were made of deer or buffalo hide. His hair was long and his skin dark and weathered. Stuck in his leather belt were a knife and one or two pistols. Around his neck hung a bullet pouch. A powder horn was slung beneath his right arm, and at least one good rifle was always in his hand or close by.

Sometimes, when the country was especially dangerous, the mountain men wore deerskin overshirts that covered them from their chins to their knees. When these shirts were soaked in water and then dried, they became so hard that they couldn't be pierced by Indian arrows.

A mountain man usually worked entirely on his own, selling his furs to the highest bidder. In rare cases he might work for one of the large fur-trading companies, and then his furs would belong to that company. Normally, however, a mountain man was a free trapper who worked alone or with only one or two companions.

For many years mountain men searched the wilderness for beaver and other animals. They learned almost everything there was to know about the mountains. They blazed trails far and wide as they set their traps in streams from the frozen north to the deserts of Mexico and into the remotest mountains.

Most mountain men had a *cache* (pronounced cash, a French word that means "hiding place") where they kept their furs until they were ready to make the long trip to a trading post. The cache was usually a hole dug in the ground and covered with grass, branches, and leaves. It had to be well made to keep its contents dry and safe from thieves and wild animals.

Then in 1825 the Rocky Mountain Fur Company changed the fur-trading business by holding a meeting, called a *rendezvous* (a French word that means "meeting place"), deep in the heart of beaver country. For the first time, a fur company was coming to the trappers instead of the other way around. At this meeting the company bought furs from the trappers and sold them rifles, powder, blankets, traps, coffee, and sugar. The trappers were able to trade their year's supply of furs for a year's supply of the things they needed. The rendezvous changed the mountain man's way of life. No longer was it necessary for them to travel hundreds of miles to a trading post to sell their furs.

The rendezvous was a great success. At its close, 8,900 pounds of beaver pelts were on their way to St. Louis, Missouri. Before the meeting ended, a second one was planned for the next summer, and a rendezvous was held every summer after that for the next ten years. To these later meetings came not only mountain men, but whole Indian tribes and traders from all the fur companies, turning the rendezvous into a lively social event with shooting matches, horse races, gambling, card games, and plenty of food and drink.

At night stories were told and new discoveries shared around the campfires. At that first rendezvous in 1825, mountain man Jim Bridger told of seeing sea birds on his way down the Bear River. He had followed them and discovered the Great

Salt Lake in Utah. At the 1828 rendezvous, another mountain man, Bill Sublette, told of finding a place where water shot from the ground, hissing and billowing. He had discovered the area in Wyoming now known as Yellowstone National Park.

Today highways and railroads follow the old trails made by the mountain men. Their camping spots have turned into great cities. The mountain men helped open the wilderness for an expanding country.

XIV

The Heavy Pants of Mr. Strauss

On January 24, 1848, gold was discovered at Sutter's Mill in California. Almost overnight people were coming to California by the thousands, hoping to make a fortune in the new gold fields. In one year San Francisco grew from a small town to a city of 25,000 people. By 1850 the territory had a population of almost 100,000, and in that year California became the thirty-first state.

The new miners needed many things, and usually they had the money to buy whatever they wanted. This abundance of people with money to spend brought a great number of peddlers and merchants to California. One of these peddlers was a man named Levi Strauss.

In 1850 Levi Strauss made the long trip from the east coast to California by boat. The trip took him all the way around the southern tip of South America. With him, Levi Strauss brought yards and yards of heavy canvas to make tents for the miners and covers for their wagons.

However, when Strauss arrived in California, he found that the miners needed good, heavy pants much more than they needed tents. None of the pants available were tough enough to stand up against the rocks of the California hills and the hard mining life. So Levi, seeing the possibility for a good business, made his tent canvas into pants instead of tents.

Strauss's tent canvas was a bit stiff for pants, so he began to make his pants out of a tough but less stiff material that he had sent to him from Nimes, France. The material was called *serge de Nimes*. Serge

is a kind of material, de means "from," and Nimes is the name of a city in France. Soon *serge* was dropped from the name, and the material was called *de Nimes*, or "denim."

The miners liked the denim pants so much that Levi couldn't make them fast enough. In fact, his pants were so well made that their basic design hasn't changed in over 100 years. Somewhere along the way they came to be called by their maker's first name—"Levi's."

Today the company that Levi Strauss began during the 1860s is still making the same basic straight-legged, button-fly, denim pants that he originally designed for the miners of California. Levi's have become so popular that they are sold (and copied) all over the world.

XV

What's in a Name?

The first chapter of this book told about the state that almost existed—Franklin, named in honor of Benjamin Franklin. It was not unusual to name a state after a famous person. Several of our states' names came about in this way—Georgia (after King George), Louisiana (after Louis XIV), and Washington (after George Washington), to name just a few. But many more states, over half of them in fact, have names that are of Indian origin.

North American Indians—the first Americans—had great respect for the land on which they lived. The names they gave to the natural objects around them not only showed this respect, but demonstrated the beauty of their languages as well.

The Sioux named the great river that runs down the center of the United States Mississippi, which means "the father of waters." From this river came the name for the state of Mississippi. Ohio was originally an Iroquois word for "great river," and Connecticut came from the Mohegan name for the Connecticut River, which meant "the long tidal river." Then there are Michigan, an Indian word meaning "a great body of water," Nebraska, an Oto word for "flat water," and Minnesota, a combination of two Sioux words meaning "sky-tinted water."

Although the Indians were not directly responsible for the word, Indiana was so named because people thought of it as the land of the Indians. Illinois, Kansas, Arkansas, Iowa, the Dakotas, and Utah were named for the tribes found in those areas. Not only was Iowa named for a local tribe, its nickname, the Hawkeye State, also has an Indian origin: Black Hawk, a Sauk Indian, was a great leader.

Wisconsin is a Chippewa word meaning "the gathering of waters." Arizona probably comes from a Papago word meaning "few springs." Wyoming means "upon the great plain," and Missouri means "people of the long canoes." Idaho is said to have come from Shoshoni for "the sun comes down the mountain." What colorful pictures each name paints of its individual state.

Kentucky is known to be of Indian origin too, but historians disagree on its exact meaning. Some have said it means "dark and bloody ground," others that it is simply a word for prairie or meadowlands. And don't forget Massachusetts, which came from the Algonkian for "near a great hill," or Tennessee, named after one of the main Cherokee villages in the region.

From the Choctaw language came two

state names, Alabama, meaning "I make a clearing," and Oklahoma, from two words meaning "red" and "people."

The names of our two largest states, Alaska and Texas, are also Indian in origin. Alaska is an Aleut word for "great land," and Texas is from the Caddo language and means "friends."

All these beautiful state names, as well as the names of many of our cities and rivers, are constant reminders of the spices that those first Americans added to America.

About the Author

"My love of history may have come from our having lived in eleven of the United States, two countries in Europe, and one South American country," says June Swanson, who now lives in Steamboat Springs, a quiet Colorado mountain town surrounded by national forests.

Ms. Swanson earned her B.A. in English at the University of Texas. A former elementary school teacher, she now teaches writing at Colorado Mountain College. Hundreds of her short stories and articles have been published in children's magazines, but this is her first book.

When she's not at the typewriter, Ms. Swanson enjoys skiing during the winter and hiking and backpacking during the summer.